엘리트 시선 64

눈꽃이 흩날릴 때
When the snowflakes fall

장 현 경 시집
Jang Hyunkyung's poetry

엘리트출판사 Elite Publisher

아름다운 꽃들의 이야기 7

눈꽃이 흩날릴 때

장현경 시집

- 서문(序文)

아름다운 꽃들의 이야기 7

나뭇잎마다 서리가 하얗게 내린 이른 아침 모자를 눌러쓰고 운동 삼아 산책하니, 허허로운 자리마다 눈에 들어오는 눈꽃. 아침을 열며 눈이 시리도록 아름다운 서리꽃이 반긴다.

프랑스의 철학자 '미셸 푸코'가 말하기를, '자기 생각을 모르기 때문에 글을 쓴다.'고 했다. 사실 글을 쓰기 전에는 내가 어떤 생각을 하고 있는지 알지 못할 뿐 아니라 공허한 마음이 가득할 뿐이다. 시인은 끊임없는 담금질로 복잡한 현실을 초월하여 순수한 감성의 세계로 몰입해야 한다는 의미일 것이다.

'글을 쓰는 사람에게 치매란 절대 없다.' 어디선가 읽고 듣고 하는 구절이다. 이는 글을 열심히 쓰라는 문구가 아닌가! 무엇인가에 몰두하다 보면, 건강에 도움이 된다는 말일 것이다. 시는 곧 삶이다. 즉 인간 삶을 바탕으로 심금을 울리는 작품을 쓰는 일이 아닌가 한다. 이런 의미에서 꽃들의 이야기는 인간 삶을 묘사하려는 듯 기쁨, 그리움, 아픔, 아름다움, 행복, 사랑 등을 주제로 삼고 있다.

    꽃을 보니 눈이 시원해지고 마음도 밝아지고 기분마저 좋아진다. 시인으로 움츠린 몸에 기지개를 켜며 사계절 지지 않는 꽃들의 이야기를 소재로 여기 한 권의 영역 시집을 다듬는다. 꽃들의 이야기가 이 어려운 시대를 견뎌내는 수많은 독자에게 위로와 희망, 감동이 되기를 기대한다.

    늘 따뜻한 성원을 보내주신 가족과 이웃의 지지에 고마운 마음 전하며 청계문학 가족 여러분의 건승을 빕니다. 나의 시편들을 만나는 존경하는 독자님께 건강과 행운이 늘 함께하시기를 기원합니다.

2024년 12월 청계서재(淸溪書齋)에서
자정(紫井) 장현경(張鉉景) 근정(謹呈)

- Preface

The Story of Beautiful Flowers 7

In the early morning, when every leaf is covered in white frost, I put on my hat and go for a walk for exercise, and snow flowers catch my eye in every empty space. As I open the morning, beautiful frost flowers greet me, making my eyes dazzle.

French philosopher Michel Foucault said, "I write because I don't know what I think." In fact, before I write, I don't know what I'm thinking, and my mind is just full of emptiness. This probably means that a poet must transcend complex reality through constant pickling and immerse himself in a world of pure emotion.

There is absolutely no dementia for those who write.' This is a phrase that I have read and heard somewhere. Isn't this a phrase that tells me to write diligently? It probably means that if I focus on something, it is good for my health. Poetry is life itself. In other words, isn't it writing a work that touches the heart based on human life? In this sense, the story of flowers seems to describe human life, using themes such as joy, longing, pain, beauty, happiness, and love.

Seeing flowers refreshes my eyes, brightens my heart, and improves my mood. I stretch my body as a poet and refine a book of poems translated into English here with the story of flowers that do not fade in the four seasons. It is hoped that the story of flowers will provide comfort, hope, and inspiration to many readers who are enduring these difficult times.

I would like to express my gratitude to the support of my family and neighbors who have always given me warm support, and wish the Cheonggye Literature family all the best. To my dear readers who meet my psalms, I wish you good health and good fortune.

December 2024 in Cheonggye Library
Jajeong, Jang Hyunkyung Raising

- 축하의 글

꽃을 노래하는 시향을 사랑하며

이 종 규 (시인, 문학평론가)

　초겨울 눈꽃이 향기롭게 흩날립니다. 수북이 쌓이는 첫눈이 나뭇가지마다 꽃을 피우며 절묘한 설경을 그려냅니다. 때맞추어 꽃을 소재로 한 장현경 작가님의 시집 『눈꽃이 흩날릴 때』가 탄생하니 참으로 놀랍고 기쁩니다. 숨겨 둔 꽃을 예술적인 가치로 승화시킨 작품을 만날 기대로 가슴이 두근거립니다.

　작가님은 이번에 일곱 번째 꽃 시집을 출간합니다. 그야말로 대한민국의 자랑스러운 '꽃 시인'입니다. 지금까지 꽃 시집을 포함한 시집, 수필집, 평론집을 모두 17권이나 발간하였습니다. 시인님은 이 많은 작품을 통해서 예술을 사랑하고 아름다운 욕구를 창조하면서 매력적이고 윤택한 삶을 추구합니다. 이번 시집에서도 유연한 생각의 온도가 겨울을 녹이는 공감의 꽃으로 장식하리라 봅니다.

 우리는 역사에 머물다 가면서 과거를 돌아봐야 미래를 그릴 수 있습니다. 시인의 눈빛은 미래를 채울 꽃을 바라보듯 언제나 그윽합니다. 매일 낯선 생각의 작품을 그리고, 매주 후배 양성을 위한 문학 특강을 하면서 문학의 꽃을 피우는 주인공입니다. 또한 『청계문학』 발행인(회장)으로서 투철한 문학 정신을 실천하며 시비 건립 등 위대한 업적을 남기는 유명 문인으로 존경하고 있습니다.

 요즈음 세상에 부는 바람은 차갑고 사람들의 마음도 아픕니다. 이럴 때 꽃을 노래하는 시향은 우리 가슴을 따뜻하게 보듬어 줄 것입니다. 빛나는 시편들이 영롱한 꽃향기로 넘치면서 예쁜 마음이 애독하는 시집으로 사랑받기를 기원합니다. 장현경 문학평론가님의 시집 발간을 축하드립니다. 감사합니다.

- congratulatory note

I Love the Scent of Singing Flowers

Yee Jonggyu literary critic

Early winter, snow flowers are fluttering fragrantly. The first snow that piles up in large quantities blooms on each tree branch, creating an exquisite snowy landscape. It is truly surprising and delightful that the poetry collection 『When Snow Flowers Fall』 by Jang Hyun-kyung, which uses flowers as its subject, has been published just in time. My heart is pounding with anticipation at the prospect of encountering a work that sublimates hidden flowers into artistic value.

The author is publishing his seventh flower poetry collection this time. He is truly the proud 'flower poet' of Korea. He has published a total of 17 poetry collections including flower poetry collections, essay collections, and critique collections. Through these many works, the poet pursues a charming and affluent life while loving art and creating beautiful desires. I believe that in this poetry collection, the temperature of flexible thoughts will decorate the winter with flowers of sympathy.

We must stay in history and look back on the past to draw the future. The poet's eyes are always profound, as if looking at flowers that will fill the future. He is the protagonist who draws works of unfamiliar thoughts every day and gives special lectures on literature every week to nurture juniors, making literature bloom. He is also a famous writer who practices a thorough literary spirit as the publisher (chairman) of 『Cheonggye Literature』 and leaves behind great achievements such as the establishment of a poetry monument.

The wind blowing through the world these days is cold and people's hearts are also hurting. At times like this, the scent of poetry that sings of flowers will warm our hearts. I hope that the shining poems will be loved as a poetry collection that pretty hearts will love to read while overflowing with the splendid scent of flowers. I congratulate literary critic Jang Hyeon-gyeong on the publication of her poetry collection. Thank you.

- 서시(序詩)

첫 눈꽃

겨울밤 추위에
첫눈이 내리네

갈색빛 풍경을
하얗게 만든 추위가
마음을 설레게 하네

낙엽마저
떠나가 버리고

가녀린 나뭇가지에
소복이 쌓여
눈꽃을 피우네!

– Opening poem

First Snow Flower

In the cold of winter night
The first snow is falling

Brown landscape
The cold that made it white
It makes my heart flutter

Even the fallen leaves
Just leave and go away

On a slender tree branch
Snow piled up
The snow flowers are blooming!

contents

□ 서문(序文): 아름다운 꽃들의 이야기 7
 (The Story of Beautiful Flower 7) ··· *004*

□ 축하의 글: 꽃을 노래하는 시향을 사랑하며
 (I Love the Scent of Singing Flowers) ··· *008*

□ 서시(序詩): 첫 눈꽃(First Snow Flower) ··· *012*

제 1부 부겐빌레아꽃

루드베키아꽃(Ludvekia Flower) ··· *020*

회화나무꽃(Pagoda Tree Flower) ··· *022*

분홍 낮 달맞이꽃(Pink Evening Primrose) ··· *024*

버베나꽃(Verbena Flower) ··· *026*

에키네시아꽃(Echinacea Flower) ··· *030*

메밀꽃(Buckwheat Flower) ··· *032*

불로초꽃(Herb of Eternal Youth Flower) ··· *036*

어리연꽃(Lotus Flower) ··· *038*

눈꽃이 흩날릴 때

오이풀꽃(A Cucumber Flower) ··· *040*

부겐빌레아꽃(Bougainvillea Flower) ··· *042*

제 2부 황화 코스모스꽃

게발선인장꽃(Crab cactus Flower) ··· *046*

개싸리꽃(Fern Flower) ··· *048*

각시취꽃(Each Odor Flower) ··· *050*

산박하꽃(Mountain Peppermint Flower) ··· *052*

감국꽃(A Persimmon Flower) ··· *056*

황화 코스모스꽃(Yellow Cosmos Flower) ··· *060*

해국꽃(Sea Aster Flower) ··· *062*

라눙쿨루스꽃(Ranunculus Flower) ··· *064*

촛불 맨드라미꽃(Candlelight Mandrami Flowers) ··· *066*

가우라꽃(Gaura Flower) ··· *068*

contents

제3부 알스트로메리아꽃

겹벚꽃(Double Cherry Blossom) ··· *072*

등나무꽃(Rattan Flower) ··· *074*

꽃향유꽃(Flower Fragrant Oil Flower) ··· *078*

한국 국화(Korean Chrysanthemum) ··· *080*

고추나물꽃(Pepper Plant Flower) ··· *084*

개다래꽃(Stem Vine Flower) ··· *086*

기름나물꽃(An Oil-Based Vegetable Flower) ··· *088*

알스트로메리아꽃(Alstroemeria Flower) ··· *092*

하이브리드 티 로즈꽃(Hybrid Tea Rose Flower) ··· *094*

겨울꽃(Winter Flowers) ··· *096*

눈꽃이 흩날릴 때

제4부 시계꽃

칼란디바꽃(Calandiva Flower) ··· *100*

시계꽃(Clock Flower) ··· *102*

당근꽃(Carrot Flower) ··· *104*

천일홍꽃(Zinnia Flower) ··· *106*

바나나꽃(Banana Flower) ··· *108*

비누꽃(Soap Flowers) ··· *110*

소철꽃(Sago Palm Flower) ··· *112*

달개비꽃(Moonflower) ··· *114*

수국꽃(Hydrangea Flower) ··· *116*

익모초꽃(Motherwort Flower) ··· *118*

contents

제5부 미들미스트 카멜리아꽃

금불초꽃(Golden Buddha Flower) ··· 122

깽깽이풀꽃(Wildflower) ··· 124

앵무부리꽃(Parrot beak Flower) ··· 126

타이탄 아룸꽃(Titan Arum Flower) ··· 128

서리꽃(Frost Flower) ··· 132

미들미스트 카멜리아꽃(Middlemist Camellia Flower) ··· 134

노랑보라 레이디 슬리퍼 난꽃(Yellow Purple Lady Slippers Orchid Flower) ··· 136

족두리꽃(Flower of the primrose) ··· 138

바다는 꽃(The Sea is a Flower) ··· 140

프로펠러꽃(Propeller Flower) ··· 142

제1부

부겐빌레아꽃

지상 어디에나
없는 곳이 없는 정열의 꽃

루드베키아꽃

바람에 흩날리는
루드베키아꽃

황금색 꽃잎과
반짝이는 검은 색 눈동자로
화단을 빛내고

해바라기와 코스모스를 닮은
여름꽃 중의 하나

인디언 처녀와 백인 장교의 사랑
죽음으로써 꽃을 피웠네

영원한 행복으로
누구에게 선물해도
어울리는 루드베키아꽃.

Ludvekia Flower

Blowing in the wind
Ludvekia flower

With golden petals
With sparkling black eyes
Brighten up the flower bed

Resembling sunflowers and cosmos
One of the summer flowers

Love between an Indian girl and a white officer
Bloomed through death

To eternal happiness
Whoever you give it as a gift
Matching Rudbeckia flowers.

회화나무꽃

마을 근처에 심는다

한여름
황백색의 꽃이
나무 전체를 뒤덮는다

목재는 건축재로 쓰이며
한국에서는 행운의 나무로
쓰인다

수령 수백 년의 회화나무
마을을 지키는 정자나무로
지정되어

천연기념물로
보호받고 있다.

Pagoda Tree Flower

Plant near the village

Midsummer
Yellowish white flowers
Cover the entire tree

Wood is used as a building material
In Korea, it is called a lucky tree.
It's used

A pagoda tree hundreds of years old
As a zelkova tree that protects the village
Designated

As a natural monument
Is protected.

분홍 낮 달맞이꽃

꽃이 많이 피니
향기도 진하고

한번 심어
오래 볼 수 있는 꽃

보이지 않게
말없이 사랑을 노래하는
관상용 화초

여리여리한 모습 보여주고 싶어
낮에 꽃이 피고
저녁에 지는
낮 달맞이꽃

꽃잎이 넓고
향이 좋아
누구나 가까이하네!

Pink Evening Primrose

There are a lot of flowers blooming
The scent is strong too

Plant it once
Flowers that can be seen for a long time

Invisible
Singing love without words
Ornamental plants

I want to show you my delicate appearance
Flowers bloom during the day
Set in the evening
A day-time moonflower

The petals are wide
It smells good
Everyone is getting closer!

버베나꽃

30cm의 키
향수의 원료로 쓰이는
앙증맞은 꽃

가위로 잘라주면
새로 번식되는 꽃

삽목이 잘 되고
꿀이 많아
예쁘게 오래가는 꽃

잎은 버들잎
말의 채찍을 닮은 줄기
버들마편초

단결로
당신의 소원이
이루어지는 버베나꽃

평원에 이룬
잊지 못할 추억
아름다운 보랏빛 꽃바다.

Verbena Flower

30cm tall
Used as a raw material for perfume
A lovely flower

If you cut it with scissors
Newly growing flowers

The cuttings are growing well
There's a lot of honey
Beautiful long lasting flowers

The leaves are willow leaves
A stem that resembles a horse's whip
Willow dandelion

In unity
Your wish
Verbena flowers that are made

Made on the plain
Unforgettable memory
A beautiful sea of purple flowers.

에키네시아꽃

1.5m의 키
꽃송이 중앙에
뾰족한 갈색 꽃술이 있고

북아메리카 원산지에
건강을 위한 약초로 쓰여
심혈관 질환 예방과
면역력 강화에 도움을 준다

면역 시스템을 자극하여
감기의 발생률과
염증 반응을 줄인다

상처 치유를 촉진하고
노화 촉진을 늦춘다

말린 뿌리나
잎을 이용해
차로 마실 수 있네!

Echinacea Flower

1.5m tall
In the center of the flower bud
It has pointed brown stamens.

Native to North America
Used as a herbal medicine for health
Prevention of cardiovascular disease and
Helps strengthen immunity

Stimulates the immune system
The incidence of colds and
Reduces inflammatory response

Promotes wound healing
Slows down the aging process

Dried roots or
Using leaves
You can drink it with tea!

메밀꽃

가을 문턱에서 보는

메밀꽃

멀리서 보니
참으로 아름답다

가까이서 보니
예쁘다

오밀조밀 피어있는
메밀꽃

자세히 보니
더욱 예쁘다

척박한 땅에서도
잘 자라
연인처럼
바람에 흩날리며
사랑을 약속한다

그리운 메밀국수
메밀냉면을 그리며.

Buckwheat Flower

From the threshold of autumn

Buckwheat flower

From a distance,
Be truly beautiful

When I looked closely
Pretty

Densely blooming
Buckwheat flower

On closer inspection,
Be even prettier

Even in the barren land
Grow up well
Like a lover
Scattered by the wind,
I promise you love

Nostalgic buckwheat noodles
I miss buckwheat cold noodles.

불로초꽃

멕시코가 원산지인
관상용 꽃

봄에서 가을까지 피는
실 모양의 한해살이 국화꽃

꺾꽂이가 잘 되어
보라와 흰색으로
싱싱한 꽃을
피우는 불로화(不老花)

군락을 이루어
피는 불로초꽃

생명력이 강해
믿음을 주며
시화(詩畫)를 떠올리게 하는
아름다운 꽃.

Herb of Eternal Youth Flower

Native to Mexico
Ornamental flowers

From spring to autumn
An annual chrysanthemum flower in the shape of a thread

With a good cut
Purple and white
Fresh flowers
Efflorescent eternal youth flower

Form a colony
Blooming fireweed flower

It has a lot of vitality
Giving us faith
Evoke the painting of poetry
A beautiful flower.

어리연꽃

여러해살이 수생식물로
줄기는 가늘고
관상용으로 인기가 높아

수심에 따라
물을 정화하고
하얀 별이 내려앉은 듯
깨달음을 상징하는 꽃

신비스럽게
물 위로 떠다녀
연꽃보다
작은 연꽃

둥근 심장 모양의 이파리
오전에 피는 순결한 꽃

청순한 잎은
약재로 쓰여
소화 기능을 활성화하고
갈증을 풀어주네!

Lotus Flower

A perennial aquatic plant
The stem is thin
It is popular for ornamental purposes.

According to depth
Purify the water
it is like a white star descending,
A flower symbolizing enlightenment.

Mysteriously
Floating on the water
Than a lotus flower
Small lotus flower

Round heart shaped leaves
Pure flowers that bloom in the morning

The innocent leaves
Are used as medicine
Activating the digestive function
And quenching thirst!

오이풀꽃

1.5m의 키에
육중한 몸체

한여름 무더위에
검붉은 색깔로
피는
강인한 꽃송이

그 옛날
오이풀 달여 먹고
항균 작용으로

만성 피로
이겨내고
전투에 임하는 병사들

그 옆에
아름다운 오이풀꽃이 있어
신선의 세계를 그린다.

A Cucumber Flower

At 1.5m tall
Heavy body

In the midsummer heat
In dark red
Blooming
A hardy flower

Back in the old days
Eat cucumber soup
With antibacterial action

Chronic fatigue
Overcome
Soldiers going into battle

Next to it
There are beautiful cucumber flowers
Draws a picture of a fairy world.

부겐빌레아꽃

에게해 섬들
인접한 정열의 나라
하얀 집
하얀 담장
하얀 부겐빌레아꽃

봄 여름 가을에 피고
베란다
화분에 심은 꽃 속의 꽃
겨울에도 피어

지상 어디에나
없는 곳이 없는
정열의 꽃

그곳에
오늘도 가 보고 싶다.

Bougainvillea Flower

Aegean islands
A neighboring country of passion
A white house
A White fence
A White bougainvillea flower

Blooms in spring, summer and fall
Veranda
A flower in a flowerpot
It blooms in the winter, too

Everywhere on earth
In every place
A flower of passion

There
I want to go there again today.

눈꽃이 흩날릴 때

제2부

황화 코스모스꽃

황야의 들판
군락을 지어
활짝 핀 황화 코스모스꽃

게발선인장꽃

내 삶의 촉을 틔워
게의 발을 흉내 내며
사막의 길을 가고 있다

불타는 사랑은
붉은 꽃으로 분출하여
멈출 줄을 몰라

내일을 소망하며

이슬 한 방울에
갈증을 해소하고

공기 정화용으로
생존을 영위하네!

Crab cactus Flower

Light up my life
Imitating the feet of a crab
I'm walking on a desert road

The burning love is
In red flowers
I don't know how to stop

Wishing for tomorrow

In a drop of dew
To quench one's thirst

For air purification
You're making a living!

개싸리꽃

높이 1m로 자라는
여러해살이풀

광주리와 빗자루로
사용되는 생활용품

꽃이 시들면
바로 낙화하지 않고
퇴색한 후에도
붙어 있다

줄기는 튼튼한데
곧게 서질 않고
인사를 하려는 듯
비스듬히 자라며

독특한 모습으로
화병이나 화환으로
잘 쓰이는
축제의 꽃.

Fern Flower

Grows to 1m tall
Perennial grass

With a basket and broom
Household goods used

When the flowers wither
I don't want to fall in love right away
Even after fading out
Be attached to

The stem is strong
Without standing straight
As if to say hello
Growing obliquely

In a unique way
With a vase or a wreath
Well used
The flower of a festival.

각시취꽃

산과 들
양지바른 곳에
흔하게 자라는
국화과의 두해살이풀로
잡초 발생을 억제한다

줄기는 곧추서며
세로로 줄이 있고
홍갈색을 띠며
잔털이 있는 야생 풀꽃

각시취는 약용으로
다양하게 쓰인다

자주색이나
진한 분홍색의 화려한 꽃이
화장한 신부 같다고 해서
붙여진 이름으로
연정을 느끼게 한다.

Each Odor Flower

The mountains and fields
In the sun
Common-growing
A biennial plant of the Asteraceae family
Suppresses weed growth

The stem is straight
There's a vertical line
With a reddish brown tone
Wild grass with hairs

Each flavor is for medicinal purposes
Be used in a variety of ways

Purple or
A colorful pink flower
Because they said I looked like a bride with makeup on
Under the name given to
It makes you feel a love interest.

산박하꽃

산에서 자라니
토종 산박하
박하라고 불리기도

산박하꽃
여러해살이풀로
자세히 보니 귀엽다

어린 순은 나물로 먹고
한 송이씩 보니
자잘한 꽃 사랑스럽다

잎의 생김새는
들깻잎을 닮았고

여름이 오면
긴 목을 빼고
자주색 꽃을 피우지만

세월이 흘러
향기 잃어버린 산박하
추억이 그립다.

Mountain Peppermint Flower

Growing up in the mountains
Native mountain mint
It's also called mint

Mountain peppermint flower
A perennial plant
It looks cute when you look closely

Young shoots are eaten as greens.
I looked at them one by one
Small flowers are lovely

The shape of the leaves
It resembles a sesame leaf

When summer comes
With a long neck
It blooms purple flowers

As time goes by
Wild peppermint that lost its scent
I miss the memories.

감국꽃

국화과에 속하는
다년생 감국꽃
한약재로 다가온다

아시아 원산지로
노란빛의 꽃송이
향기가 진하고

단맛이 나는 꽃잎
불로장생을 돕고
재앙을 막아 주네

기침이 날 때
감국차는
향기와 맛으로
피로를 풀어 준다

꽃을 따서
술에 넣어 마시고

가을 향기가 은은하게
스며드는 감국꽃
가을의 정취가
노랗게 퍼져가네!

A Persimmon Flower

Belonging to the Asteraceae family
Perennial persimmon flower
Approaching as a herbal medicine

In Asian origin
A yellow flower
With a strong scent

Sweet petals
To help you live eternal life
He's preventing disaster

When you cough
Gamguk tea is
With scent and taste
Relieve one's fatigue

After picking flowers
I don't want you to put it in the alcohol

It has a soft autumn scent
An oozing persimmon flower
The mood of autumn
It's spreading yellow!

황화 코스모스꽃

가을 날씨

하늘은 높고
아름다운 구름 아래

황화 코스모스꽃
싱싱하고 예쁘게 피어
눈을 뗄 수 없다

황야의 들판
군락을 지어
활짝 핀 황화 코스모스꽃

넘치는 야성미에
황금빛 물결을 이루어
기쁨을 누리고 있다.

Yellow Cosmos Flower

Autumn weather

The sky is high
Under a beautiful cloud

A yellow cosmos flower
It's fresh and pretty
Can't take one's eyes off

A field in the wilderness
In a colony
Full bloom yellow cosmos flowers

Full of wildness
In a golden wave
Enjoy one's pleasure.

해국꽃

바위틈 사이에 핀
해국꽃

가을이 왔다는 듯이
국화와 어우러져
활짝 피었네

베란다
정원
가로수길
교회 가는 길
바닷가
연못가
낙엽이 뒹구는 길에도

국화꽃과 경쟁하듯이
화사하게 피었네

해국꽃
누구를 기다리고 있을까?

Sea Aster Flower

Blooming between the rocks
A sea aster flower

As if fall is here
In harmony with the chrysanthemums
It's in full bloom

Veranda
Garden
Garosu-gil Road
On the way to church
The beach
By the pond
Even on the road where fallen leaves are rolling around

Like competing with chrysanthemum flowers
It's bright

Sea aster flower
Who am I waiting for?

라눙쿨루스꽃

미나리 같은 줄기에
장미를 닮은 라눙쿨루스
봄을 아는 듯
예쁘게 꽃이 핀다

매혹적이다
크림색 도는 꽃
꽃잎이 300장

색상마다
무척 화려한 인상을 주어
애지중지 보고 싶었던 꽃

와!
그대는 꽃 중의 여왕!

Ranunculus Flower

On the stem like a water parsley
Ranunculus, which resembles a rose
Like you know spring
Flowers bloom beautifully

Be fascinating
Creamy flowers
300 petals

For each color
To give a very fancy impression
A flower I've been longing for

Wow!
You are the queen of flowers!

촛불 맨드라미꽃

산들바람이
황야에 피는
촛불 맨드라미를
흔들고

갖가지 색상으로
나부끼는
촛불 맨드라미꽃

예쁘고 화려하게
강한 생명력이 느껴지는
열정의 숨소리

작은 촛불이
올망졸망
서로 사랑하듯
그리움을 담고 있네!

Candlelight Mandrami Flowers

The breeze
Blooming in the wilderness
Candle mandrami
Shake it

In a variety of colors
Fluttering
Candlelight mandrami flowers

Pretty and glamorous
With a strong sense of vitality
The breath of passion

A small candle
All-mansolmang
Like we love each other
It contains longing!

가우라꽃

길가에 핀
조그마한 꽃송이들

자세히 보면
참으로 예쁘다

바람에 흔들흔들
산야에 핀 야생화

멀리서 보면
나비가 팔랑이는 듯

여기저기
오래오래 꽃이 피어

아름다운 여인이
떠나간 이를 그리워하듯
춤을 추네!

Gaura Flower

Blooming on the side of street
Small flower buds

If you look closely
It's very pretty

Swaying in the wind
Wild flowers blooming in the wild

From a distance
Like a butterfly fluttering

All over the place
The flowers will bloom for a long time

A beautiful woman
Like I miss the one who left
She's dancing!

눈꽃이 흩날릴 때

제3부

알스트로메리아꽃

겨우내 길목에서
졸업 입학의 축하 꽃다발로
그대는 탄생한다.

겹벚꽃

몽글몽글하고
탐스러운 겹벚꽃

여러 겹으로 겹쳐 피어
풍성하고 아름답다

이름만 들어도
설레는 마음

싱그러운 봄기운으로
흰색과 분홍색이
섞여 피어
장관을 연출한다

때로는
연둣빛 산이
배경이 되어
더욱 사랑스러운 겹벚꽃
사람의 발길을 잡는다.

Double Cherry Blossom

Fuzzy and hazy
A coveted double cherry blossom

Peering in layers
Be rich and beautiful

Just by the name of it
A fluttering heart

With the fresh spring spirit
White and pink
A mixed bloom
Create a spectacular scene

At times
A light green mountain
In the background
More lovely double cherry blossoms
Catch a person's feet.

등나무꽃

화려한 꽃과 향기를
지닌 등나무꽃
가던 발길을 멈추게 한다

10m의 키
100년의 수명
꽃송이는 1m
갖가지 색상의 꽃이
2주 내내 피어 있다

덩굴식물로
울타리로
주변 경관을 꾸미고
그늘을 만들어
시각적인 흥미를 유발한다

등나무꽃은
봄을 대표하는 꽃으로
향기롭고 아름다워
사람들에게 사랑을 받는 꽃

등나무 꽃차로
기침과 가래를 삭인다.

Rattan Flower

The colorful flowers and scents
A wisteria flower with a crown of thorns
Stops your steps

10m tall
100 years of life
A flower is 1m long
Flowers of various colors
Be in bloom for two weeks

With vines
With a fence
Decorating the surrounding landscape
Let's make a shade
To arouse visual interest

The rattan flower
A flower that represents spring
It's fragrant and beautiful
A beloved flower

With a wisteria flower tea
It cures cough and phlegm.

꽃향유꽃

산과 들에 피어
은근히 예쁜
꽃향유꽃

가을 향기가 그리운
보랏빛 꽃향유

단풍이 예쁘게
물드는 계절에

찾아오는
기침감기에
좋은

꽃향유 꽃차
행운을 부르네!

Flower Fragrant Oil Flower

Blooming in the mountains and fields
Rather pretty
Flower fragrant oil flower

I miss the scent of autumn
Purple flower fragrance

The autumn leaves are pretty
In the dyeing season

Coming
For a cold with a cough
Good

Flower tea with fragrant oil
Good luck!

한국 국화

키가 크고
줄기도 튼튼한 꽃

자주색
예쁜 꽃이
화장한 신부 같아
각시취꽃

이름만큼 예뻐
둥글둥글
귀여운 꽃송이

오래 꽃을 피워
기억에 남는 꽃

가을 야생화
위궤양에 좋은 약초

분홍 꽃잎 위에
구름처럼
어른거리는 모습
아, 한국 국화!

Korean Chrysanthemum

Tall
Flowers with strong stems

Purple
Pretty flowers
Like a bride with makeup
Korean chrysanthemum

As pretty as its name
Round
Cute flower buds

Bloom for a long time
Flowers that are memorable

Autumn Wildflowers
Good Herbs for Peptic Ulcers

On top of the pink petals

Like a cloud

Flickering

Ah, Korean Chrysanthemum!

고추나물꽃

여러해살이풀
한국의 야생화
고추나물꽃

여린 순은 나물로 먹고
꽃은 튀김과 차로 마신다

지혈 작용
해독
당뇨병
면역력
우울증
천연 비아그라
혈액순환
피부 미용
염증 제거에 효과 있는

고소득 작물.

Pepper Plant Flower

Perennial herb
Korean wildflowers
Peppermint flower

Young leaves are eaten as greens
Flowers are fried and drunk as tea

Hemostatic effect
Detoxification
Diabetes
Immunity
Depression
Natural Viagra
Blood circulation
Skin beauty
Effective in removing inflammation

High income crops.

개다래꽃

덩굴성 식물
계속 자라
줄기가 4~6m

하얀 꽃잎에
노란색 꽃술
개다래 양성화꽃

관상용으로 심어
열매는 약용하고

꽃이 피면
잎이 하얗게 변한다

영리한 개다래
통풍 중풍에 효능 있는
나무 약초

개다래꽃 가까이하면
당신을 버리지 않아요!

Stem Vine Flower

A climbing plant
Continuously growing
Stems 4~6m

White petals
Yellow stamens
Stem vine bisexual flowers

Planted for ornamental purposes
The fruit is medicinal

When the flowers bloom
The leaves turn white

Smart stem vine
Effective for gout and stroke
Wood herbs

If you get close to the stem vine flower
It won't abandon you!

기름나물꽃

갑자기
오늘의 야생화
기름나물꽃들을 만나면

식물에 기름 성분이 있어
꺾거나 비볐을 때
온몸에 달려드는 고소한 향기로
전율한다

꽃은 하얀색으로
무리 지어
사랑을 꽃피우고

꽃대 하나에
많은 꽃송이가 달려 있다

어린 새잎은
생채로 먹고

다 자란 식물은
신경통을 완화하고
가래를 멈추게 해
사랑을 고백한다.

An Oil-Based Vegetable Flower

Suddenly
Today's wild flower
When I meet oil plants

The plant has oil
When you bend or rub it
It's a savory scent that runs all over your body
I'm shivering

The flowers are white
In groups
Blooming love

On a flower stand
There are many flowers

Little young leaves
I ate it raw

The grown plants
I'll relieve my neuralgia
Stop phlegm
I confess my love.

알스트로메리아꽃

겨울에도
실외 정원에서
인간에게 흔적을 남기며
세월을 지나온다

예쁜 꽃으로 보여주고 싶어 하는
알스트로메리아꽃

시원하고 풍성하게
갖가지 색깔로 새롭게
인간과
만나고 싶어 하네

서로 사랑을 나누며
새로운 희망을 안고
겨울의 꽃으로 추천

겨우내 길목에서
졸업 입학의 축하 꽃다발로
그대는 탄생한다.

Alstroemeria Flower

Even in winter,
In the outdoor garden,
Leaving traces on humans
Passing through the years

Wanting to show off as a pretty flower
Alstroemeria flower

Cool and rich
New in various colors
With humans
He wants to meet you

Sharing love with each other
With new hope
Recommended as a winter flower

On the street this winter
With a congratulatory bouquet of graduation and entrance
You are born.

하이브리드 티 로즈 꽃

긴 줄기 끝에
크고 아름답게 피는
한 송이의 꽃

색상이 다양하고
향기가 좋은 꽃

오랫동안
사람들의 관심을
받아온 꽃

인류의 문화 예술에
뿌리내린 꽃

볼수록 더욱 반가운
하이브리드 티 로즈꽃

Hybrid Tea Rose Flower

At the end of a long stem
Big and beautifully blooming
A flower

A flower with a variety of colors
A flower with a good fragrance

For a long time
The attention of the people
Flowers received

In the culture and art of mankind
A flower with its roots

The more I see it, the more I'm glad to see it
Hybrid tea rose flower.

겨울꽃

그 길 위에 서 있는
풀과 나무 잠든 절기

천년만년
밤에 내린 눈꽃과 비조차
수빙(樹氷)으로
눈꽃 피운 나목들

군데군데 바위틈
나뭇가지 끝
계곡 물길에

눈보라 흩날리며
겨울꽃을 빚는다.

Winter Flowers

Standing on the road
The season when grass and trees sleep

Thousand years
Even the snow and rain that fell at night
With tree ice
Trees covered with snow

Cracks in the rocks here and there
The tip of a branch
In the valley stream

With the snow flurry falling
Make winter flowers.

눈꽃이 흩날릴 때

제4부

시계꽃

꽃의 모양이
시계와 같아
시계꽃

칼란디바꽃

꽃잎이 겹겹이 쌓여
봄과 잘 어울리는
칼란디바꽃

꽃이 풍성하고 아름다워
활짝 핀 모습이
설레는 기분을 준다

사랑을 고백할 때
선물하기 좋은 꽃
섬세하고
우아한 느낌을 준다

세련된 사람에게
칼란디바꽃과 함께하는 삶이
행복하기를!

Calandiva Flower

Petals piled up in layers
Goes well with spring
Calandiva flower

The flower are abundant and beautiful
The sight in full bloom
Give me an excited feeling

When you confess your love
Flower good for gifts
Delicate
Gives an elegant feeling

For sophisticated people
Life with calandiva flowers
May you be happy!

시계꽃

온실이나 화단에서 보는
여러해살이풀

남아메리카가 원산지이며
관상용으로 쓴다

꽃의 모양이
시계와 같아
시계꽃

초침 분침 시침이 있어
째깍째깍
시간이 가는 듯.

Clock Flower

Viewed from a greenhouse or flower bed
Perennial herb

It is native to South America
Used for ornamental purposes

The shape of the flower
It's like a clock
A clock flower

There is a second hand, a minute hand, and an hour hand.
Tick tock
Time seems to pass.

당근꽃

당근은 한해살이풀
꽃봉오리 맺히자

하얀색을 띠는 당근꽃
앙증스럽게 활짝 피네

비타민C와 카로텐이 풍부한
당근
영양 만점 야채

빨간 당근 뿌리
죽음도 아깝지 않으리!

Carrot Flower

Carrots are annual plants.
Flower buds form

Carrot flower with white color
Blooming brightly

Rich in vitamin C and carotene
Carrot
Nutritious vegetables

Red carrot root
I wouldn't even mind dying!

천일홍꽃

맑고 푸른 하늘 아래
노을빛이 물들 무렵에
피어난
선물 같은 한 송이 꽃

내 사랑 알알이 영글어
빨강 하양으로
아롱다롱 맺혀
옹기종기 웃는 꽃

꽃잎 한 장씩
넘길 때마다
한 몸이 되어
천년을 사는 꽃

아쉬움과 사랑
그리움의 향기가 지켜주는
인연의 꽃.

Zinnia Flower

Under a clear blue sky
When the sunset is in full effect
Bloomed
A single flower like a gift

My love is beautiful
In red and white
Arongdarong tied together
Flowers laughing together

One flower petal at a time
Every time I turn it over
Become one body
A flower that lives for a thousand years

Regret and love
The scent of longing protects you
The flower of fate.

바나나꽃

비가 그치고
햇볕이 쨍쨍

바나나꽃이 피고
열매가 열리기까지
걸리는 보름 동안의 시간

잎이 빨갛게 물들어 가면
꽃대가 올라가는 신호
꽃잎이 하나씩 펼쳐지고
열매가 열린다

꽃잎마다
바나나 뭉텅이로 열려
우리의 건강을 지키네!

Banana Flower

The rain stopped
The sun is shining brightly

Banana flowers are blooming
Until the fruit ripens
The time it takes for a fortnight

When the leaves turn red
The signal for the flower stalk to rise
The petals unfold one by one
The fruit is ripe

Each petal
Opens like a banana bunch
Protecting our health!

비누꽃

향기가 좋은 비누 향

꽃다발을 선물할 때
생화는 가격이 높고
보관이 짧기 때문에

오래 보관하고
다양하게 쓸 수 있어
비누꽃을 쓴다

그만큼 손도 씻고
급할 때
비누로 쓸 수 있어
인기가 있다.

Soap Flowers

A fragrant soap scent

When giving a bouquet of flowers
Flowers are expensive
Because the storage period is short

Keep it for a long time
It can be used in various ways
Use soap flowers

Wash your hands too
When in a hurry
You can use it as soap
It's popular.

소철꽃

저 멀리
아열대 지역에서 시집온
귀화식물

이 땅에 뿌리 내리려
비바람에
온갖 고초를 겪은 꽃

20~30년에
한 번 피는
황금빛의 꽃

강한 사랑의 화석(化石)으로
알려진 소철꽃

한 번 보기만 해도
경사스러운 일

경건한 마음으로
사랑스러운 눈빛으로
그대를 바라본다.

Sago Palm Flower

Over there
Married from a subtropical region
Naturalized plants

To put down roots in this land
In the rain and wind
A flower that has endured all kinds of hardships

In 20~30 years
Once bloomed
Golden Flower

As a fossil of strong love
Known sago palm flower

Just take a look
A sloped event

With a devout heart
With loving eyes
I look at you.

달개비꽃

가을!

달개비가 가을을
빛깔로 알리고 있다

암수한몸에
가냘픈 꽃송이

가까이 다가가
휴대폰 카메라로
한 컷 찰칵!

Moonflower

Autumn!

The moonflower is in autumn
Informing with color

In a hermaphroditic body
A delicate flower bud

Come closer
With a cell phone camera
One cut, click!

수국꽃

갖가지 색깔의 꽃

흰색과 주홍
연 핑크
연둣빛 보라

무더운 날씨에
둥글고 예쁘게 피는 꽃

꽃송이 하나씩 뭉쳐
큰 꽃이 되고
다시 단결하여
더 큰 꽃 무리를 이룬다

당당하게
그대 어여쁨
반짝반짝 빛나리!

Hydrangea Flower

Flowers of various colors

White and vermilion
Light pink
Light purple

In hot weather
Round and pretty flowers

Let's gather up one flower at a time
And become a big flower
United again
Form larger flower clusters

With confidence
You are so pretty
Shine brightly!

익모초꽃

익모초는
여성 건강에
도움을 주는
대표적인 약초

염증 완화
스트레스 해소
불면증 개선에
효과적인 약재

꽃차로 활용하거나
말려서 쓴다.

Motherwort Flower

The motherwort is
For women's health
Helpful
Representative medicinal herbs

Anti-inflammation
Stress relief
To improve insomnia
Effective medicine

Use it as a flower tea or
It is used after drying.

눈꽃이 흩날릴 때

제5부

미들미스트 카멜리아꽃

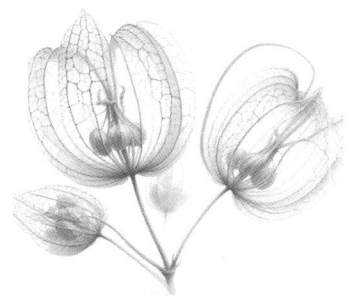

동백꽃을 닮아
심리적으로 안정을 가져오고
스트레스를 줄여준다

금불초꽃

산들바람이
나뭇잎을 흔들고

풀잎 사이를 스쳐
나부끼는 황금빛 부처꽃

노란 꽃송이마다
향기롭고
강한 생명력이 느껴지는
부처의 숨소리

금불초꽃을 보고
상큼한 하루를
그려보네!

Golden Buddha Flower

The gentle breeze
Shakes the leaves

Brushing through the grass
Fluttering golden Buddha flowers

Every yellow flower
Smells fragrant
I feel a strong vitality
The sound of Buddha's breath

Looking at the goldenrod flowers
Have a refreshing day
I'm drawing it!

깽깽이풀꽃

4월이 오면

가녀린 꽃대에
보라와 흰색으로
사랑스럽게 피는 꽃

꽃이 진 후
나오는
이파리도 귀여워

긴 꽃대가 산들바람에
한들한들

서로 사랑하며
아쉬운 마음
달래주네!

Wildflower

When April comes

On a slender flower stalk
In Purple and white
A flower that blooms lovingly

After the flowers wither
Coming out
The leaves are cute too

Long flower stems sway in the breeze
Shaking and shaking

Love each other
Regretful heart
It's soothing!

앵무부리꽃

포근한 땅에
예쁜 꽃으로 피어나

꽃 모양이
앵무새 부리와
비슷하고

꽃대가 늘어나며
꽃망울이 올망졸망

바나나 이파리와
경쟁하듯이
키 재기를 하고

열대지방이나
암벽에서
흔히 보이는 꽃.

Parrot beak Flower

In the warm land
Blooming into a pretty flowers

The shape of the flower
Parrot beak and
Similar

The flower stem grows longer
Flower buds are blooming

With banana leaves
Competitively
I'm measuring my height

In tropical regions or
On the rock
A commonly seen flower.

타이탄 아룸꽃

키는 3m
수십 년에 한 번씩
꽃을 피우는
희귀한 꽃

지독한 냄새로
인도네시아에서
자라는 '시체꽃'

알같이 생긴 꽃봉오리가
여기저기 솟아나
신기하고 두렵다

뉴욕에선
800m 떨어진 곳까지
시체 냄새를 퍼뜨려
'죽음의 꽃'이라 불린다

시체 냄새가 나는 꽃이
인기라며
구름같이
모여드는 관람객

꽃 같지 않은 꽃
볼수록 신기하여
장대한 미를 느끼게 하네!

Titan Arum Flower

Height is 3m
Once every few decades
Blooming flowers
Rare flower

With a terrible smell
In Indonesia
Growing 'Corpse Flower'

Flower buds that look like eggs
It's all over the place
It's amazing and scary

In New York
Up to 800m away
Spread the smell of a corpse
It's called the "Flower of Death."

A flower that smells like a corpse
It's popular
Like a cloud
Crowd of spectators

A flower that doesn't look like a flower
The more I look at it, the more amazing it is
It makes me feel the grand beauty!

서리꽃

나뭇잎마다
서리가 하얗게 내린
이른 아침

모자를 눌러쓰고
운동 삼아
산책하니

허허로운 자리마다
눈에 들어오는 눈꽃

아침을 열며
눈이 시리도록 아름다운
서리꽃이 반긴다.

Frost Flower

On every leaf
The frost is white
Early morning

Put your hat on
For exercise
Going for a walk

In every empty space
Snowflake in the eye

Opening the morning
So beautiful that it hurts my eyes
Frost flowers welcome you.

미들미스트 카멜리아꽃

비가 그치고
햇볕이 쨍쨍

예쁜 카멜리아꽃
미적 가치가 넘치네

강한 생명력으로
공기 정화에 도움을 주고

동백꽃을 닮아
심리적으로 안정을 가져오고
스트레스를 줄여준다

꽃이 크고 아름다워
희귀할 뿐 아니라
우리에게
환한 웃음을 주리리.

Middlemist Camellia Flower

The rain stopped
The sun is shining brightly

Pretty Camellia flower
It's overflowing with aesthetic value

With strong vitality
Helps purify the air

Resembles a camellia flower
Brings psychological stability
Reduces stress

The flowers are big and beautiful
Not only is it rare,
To us
Will give us a bright smile.

노랑보라 레이디 슬리퍼 난꽃

노랑과 보라가
어우러진 꽃

신발과 비슷한 모양
슬리퍼 난

세상에서
제일 비싸고
희귀한 꽃 중의 하나

영국에서
법으로 보호받고

미국에서는
자연보호의 대상.

Yellow Purple Lady Slippers Orchid Flower

Yellow and purple
Mixed flowers

Shape similar to a shoe
I have slippers

In the world
The most expensive
one of the rare flowers

In England
Protected by law

In the United States,
Object of nature conservation.

족두리꽃

저 멀리
중앙아메리카에서 건너온
귀화식물

한국의 기후에 적응하여
귀화에 성공한 꽃

나비 날개 같은 꽃잎
바람에 날아가는 듯

가지 끝에 피는
꽃 뭉치의 모양이
왕관과 비슷하여 왕관꽃

결혼할 때
쓰는 족두리와 비슷하여
족두리꽃.

Flower of the primrose

Over there
From Central America
Naturalized plants

Adapted to the Korean climate
A flower that succeeded in naturalization

Petals like butterfly wings
As if flying in the wind

Blooming at the tip of a branch
The shape of the flower bouquet
Crown flower, similar to a crown

When you get married
It is similar to the writing brush
Flower of the primrose.

바다는 꽃

그대는 바다
바다는 꽃
난 흘러가는 강물

바다가 좋아서
파도가 좋아서

강물은 흘러
바다로

갈매기 울음소리
내 마음인 듯

그대 미소 지으며
내 손을 잡아주네!

The Sea is a Flower

You are the sea
The sea is a flower
I am the flowing river

Because I like the sea
Because I like the waves

The river flows
To the sea

the cry of a seagull
It seems to be my heart

With your smile
Hold my hand!

프로펠러 꽃

길을 가다가 보는
예쁘고
특이한 꽃

하얀 꽃송이를
받치고 있는
긴 이파리 같은
꽃잎 날개

이전에는 필라멘트 꽃
이제는 프로펠러 꽃

프로펠러 힘으로
몸체를 움직여
앞으로 날아가네

새로
탄생한 프로펠러 꽃
영원하리.

Propeller Flower

Seen on the road
It's pretty
Unusual flower

White flower buds
Supporting
Long leaf-like
Petal wings

Formerly filamentous flowers
Now the propeller flower

With the power of a propeller
Move your body
Flying forward

Newly
Propeller flower born
Forever.

눈꽃이 흩날릴 때

초판인쇄 2024년 12월 12일 초판발행 2024년 12월 18일

지은이 장현경

펴낸이 장현경 펴낸곳 엘리트출판사

편집 디자인 마영임

등록일 2013년 2월 22일 제2013-10호

서울특별시 광진구 긴고랑로15길 11 (중곡동)

전화 010-5338-7925

E-mail : wedgus@daum.net

정가 14,000원

ISBN 979-11-87573-48-7 03810